IGUANA IGUANA

CAYLIN CAPRA-THOMAS

DEEP VELLUM

DALLAS, TEXAS

Deep Vellum Publishing
3000 Commerce St., Dallas, Texas 75226
deepvellum.org · @deepvellum

Deep Vellum is a 501c3 nonprofit literary arts organization
founded in 2013 with the mission to bring
the world into conversation through literature.

Support for this publication has been provided in part by grants from the
National Endowment for the Arts, the Texas Commission on the Arts,
the City of Dallas Office of Arts and Culture's ArtsActivate program,
and the Moody Fund for the Arts:

 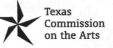 

ISBNS: 978-1646051779 (paperback) | 978-1646051762 (ebook)

Library Of Congress Control Number: 2021952051

Cover design and interior layout typesetting by Zoe Norvell

Printed in the United States of America

TABLE OF CONTENTS

III.

PASSAGE

It's hard to tell what will be important. The river

is high again and so are the teenagers encrusting

its edges, beady-eyed and black-clad, sideways

glancing, suspicious as crows. Each in the cluster

a dead version of yourself: one scratching peace

signs into the dirt with her toe. One singing

ugly. One poking a drowned worm, expressionless.

And you stand apart, head cocked, remembering

that the French for *to happen* also means *to arrive,*

that sometimes we say *deceased* when we mean

departed. The obscure chorus of your own life

keeps cawing into the diamond dark, under the roaring

of each body you inhabit, the waters, the others

you've flocked to, even when all you can hear

are your own hard swallows, or the sweet shriek

of those far-off trains you suspect are coming

to claim you. To lay open the hills you haven't seen.

I.

WINDOW

So many friends I've caught beautiful, not knowing it,

cursing me in the snow or fumbling shirtless through

cabinets for the last sachet of tea. Their petulance

an unlikely ornament. It is easier, I suppose, to wrap

myself in myself. The root of us, alone a lot. So I cook

near-naked by the kitchen window. I try so hard

to get caught. But nobody looks up while they walk

home to whatever awaits them. Not me, not this soup

of lemon and leftover stock. Perhaps the television, left on

since morning, the newscast too loud, never-ending.

Perhaps a note that says, *I'm leaving*. I've gone out and left

the stove on for hours at a time, many times. Somehow

nothing's caught fire. But I know how luck is finite,

quantifiable, and this knowledge is an under-the-skin

feeling, like being watched. Like being told how lovely

I look, bathed in the light of my own life, burning.

PATRON SAINTS

The people were not cruel, but the town was.

In its heart, it was. In its heart of mills and falls

and wind, it flogged itself, its people, who loved

God and prayed to So-and-So, patron saint of

whatever. Everyone there waiting for something

that would never return. Some had waited so long,

they forgot what it was and decided to call it heaven—

the thing they waited for, that is. The town

was not heaven but was also—sometimes,

when I think about it—not Earth.

Some other, nowhere place. Alien in its grey

and beige, its salted streets and stone walls.

Some days I'd climb to the top of the road

to the old farm where my father saw his collie's

ghost. And I'd stand there waiting to see Franz,

thinking, *It's true we all come back, everything,*

everyone returns. And when I saw nothing

but late winter's gold lick the forsaken trees

and some schoolmates tool by in an old Saturn

ringed around the rims with snow, I knew

I'd been abandoned by something, that Saint

So-and-So was sleeping, forever sleeping—leave

her be—and whatever I was waiting for lived

somewhere else and I was never coming back.

FOR MY TWENTY-YEAR-OLD SISTER ON MY THIRTIETH BIRTHDAY

Nobody knows what they're doing, Maddie.
Sometimes I can see, as if from above, the wave
of each fresh generation gathering, drawing

more of itself into itself and looming, perilous
and untenable, above the lower water.
The collective breath of newborns responsible

for the atmospheric shift. Freaky shit. The morning
shows call it sweater weather. I call it death knell
with elbow patches. *Best case scenario*, I say,

how do you think the world will end? It's near 2 a.m.
and you're walking uphill in Worcester in a silver
dress, shivering like the moon must shiver

in her lockstep tidal darkness. Know me, sister.
I bequeath you the decade between us. It was
useless and warm, like a house party.

Like a house party, I spent it in the kitchen,
counter-top-perched, glittering so lightly
no one noticed my gravity. I felt like I knew

something then. It was mostly a feeling. *Best case
scenario*? you say. *Dinosaurs return for a feeding.*

CROSSCUT

So many girls are trying to tell you this:
the line between the hurt body and the body

that hurts is razor-thin and traversable
like the trail we carved into the mountain

to climb beyond the snow line and slip off.
Pain, the happening. Pain, the procedure.

Firewood is not the tree's submission
but the consequence of being rooted.

One place will cut you down. Girls,
this is not forever. We are not forever,

but we will forever have been here.
Clear-eyed and cross-legged

in the crosscut clearing. Plain-toothed.
Champion-toothed. The woodsman

who walks the forest whistles grateful
tunes to tall specters who arrive

only in the shape of absence, apparition
of light on the needled ground

which once knew only shadow.

ONE WAY

West is always west, I was told. Direction,

not destination. That was the year everything was

small: my little finger fine-scooping powder

to my gums. It was only detergent. Tide, I think.

Maybe Cascade. Some crude and certain force.

I ate it. It cleaned me. The year moved on like water.

The year with its dried hydrangea, the year

with its cut green beans. The year with others in it—

sometimes. The sometimes with bags of oranges,

the oranges with hard little navels, the navels identical

to mine. My lives full of scattered wanting,

burnt hair, and excavation sites. Who invited

the mountains, anyway? The bear-shaped honey bottle

a long-bygone ex placed on my sill is there still,

and full. I haven't picked it up all year. Its nose

presses against the unwashed window, begs blowflies

from some hidden rot, faces always west.

PAST-LIFE SELF PORTRAIT WITH MOUNTAINS

Oh, honey. Your thoughts fermenting like vinegar, like
the flies that once burst into being behind the cupboard—
something dead back there. Montana me, everything
a poem: buttons, bottles, anything that could be
emptied or undone. Anything that could be
but wouldn't: the version of myself that stayed
and figured out how to forage for morels.
Something good from wildfire—Allison
taught me that, plus the names of the pines,
those ones that smelled sweet and whose cones
the heat busted open. (Ponderosa.) Something good
from all that fire—Montana me, you go on
somewhere, still burning it down every year, still
bursting into being in spring like flies or pines
or mushrooms. Still nervous as a ghost, throat
filled with smoke—something dead out there:
Montana me, gray wisp, whatever the fire
leaves behind.

CALLAHAN AND SUMNER

I want to be pure, unbodied rightness. The darkness

of a tunnel, or a mouth, which is a tunnel into a self

made physical, so definite: spring-loaded small

intestine, in effect infinite, long enough to journey

to the bakery and back, and it's wild how we hold

so many miles inside us, but some people die

in the same town where they were born. In the town

where I was born, my great-grandparents ran

a pizzeria-bakery, made pies as wide as their appetite,

which they passed down to my grandfather,

my mother, then me. When I say I want to be

rightness, I mean I want to be spun like dough

into the sky—precise and high. My grandfather

stuffed his with mozzarella, salami, capicola.

He ate mayonnaise with a spoon. He died

with his mouth around a harmonica, its comb

tilling ditches into his cooling lips. Long

before that, he dug tunnels under Boston—

the same ones my mother used to escape that grey-

coated city to sordid Sarasota, Florida, then again

when she returned. When I asked how she knew

where she belonged she said, *Gut feeling*.

We were traveling the tunnel her father built

towards the airport where I'd depart but not escape.

It's not an escape if nothing pursues, if there's

no one to grasp the glove you wriggle out of.

Anyway, there is rightness to a tunnel, integrity

in the dark with the bay beating down—resistance

to pressure. I want that, to be what holds people but

briefly, then the brightness that greets them at the end.

ALTER EGO WITH SHEEP

Here, I will not try to find anything.

I will not try to charm or fade
my pink ache to be liked.

I will not wander wide-eyed
the drug-store aisles searching

(supplement, salve)

the eyes of every cashier
and customer

        (supplicant, save me)

I will not be on guard. I will not
cherry-pick the argument or paint myself

hard like I like black coffee
or what pains me, can swallow

pills dry, or don't need
        (relief)

I will not be shamefaced or sheepish,

will not bleat when they don't carry
the ten-milligram melatonin

or the right under-eye brightener
to invent a night's sleep.

I will tend sheep.

Shelter, salt, straw. I will shear
sheep when they get shaggy,
keep watch for wild teeth.

I will give them my only good,
knowing we may never be remembered.

No god or guide, and so no shepherd.

Just, tender.

THE FUNNY PART

The tomato seedlings daily grow higher and I don't have the heart

to tell them I'm no gardener, crushing cigarettes into dead leaves.

I plant the filters with shaking hands, nails worried to their beds.

How are any of us to bear what we create? It's almost the first

of May and I want to say that I find all this blooming tyrannical.

The insistence of white petals I can't name. People can't stop pulling

at my mouth. *In the beginning,* they say, *clowns were always sad,*

and this is the funny part. To discuss great finalities, the bottom

lines, we begin with *At the end of the day…* It is the golden hour.

I won't mention the length of the shadows, the garden's weeds

looming, lion-headed as the inevitable sunrise over another day

alone. From the refrigerator I retrieve a bowl of store-

bought cherry tomatoes and stand before the mirror, holding one

in front of my nose, and it's funny. I sob and sob. I am practicing.

SPRING-LOADED

The droning has returned: killer wasps, lawn mowers,

the din of someone else's yard party and the contagious

yawning that accompanies everyone falling in and out

of love. Spring, I guess, and Rikka said it is funny how

at the first sight of bare skin we all turn into bonobos.

I remove my shirt and worry a burn. Wait for a man

to arrive and cup my ass with his hands. It is a loving

gesture. Maybe just one that I love. I mean a specific

man, choose an ambiguous article. I feel safer this way.

 It is just a feeling, though, like knowing that my seat

cushion turns into a flotation device. Whoever needs it

is already pretty seriously fucked. But I still want him

to sit atop my bed on a Thursday afternoon. Tip scotch

between my lips while the refrigerator repairman grunts

on his haunches in the next room. Even the appliances

are done with being good, now blowing only hot breath

over the lettuces: Bibb or Boston, the city I left without

a great deal of affection. When I return there, I feel held

in the mouth of a larger animal, the noise of the world

muzzled by a heavy tongue. Wet walls of bitten cheek.

PETE

The Florida self goes on in an alternate universe.
She lives alone, soundlessly, save for the hissing
pet snakes. They like her, she thinks, as much
as a snake likes anything. As much as frozen mice
and crickets—but not more. She thinks she looks
like a giant, frozen mouse to them, sweating
before the freezer, longing for snow.

She once kept pet mice—I did, I mean, we—
in our shared childhood. A lineage of squeakers
from Oceans of Pets, all called Mousey Mousey.
Except for Houdini, who froze half to death
when our father cut our bedroom's heat
during the week with our mother. Frantic,
he called the vet and wondered whether we'd
notice if he swapped the old, cold mouse for fresh.
Then, with the cage next to the woodstove,
Houdini sprang back to life. This was the magic
of Houdini: he rose from the dead.

The Florida self considers this when she feeds
the snakes, all called Snakey Snakey. Except
for Pete. *I don't know*, she tells her friends—
she's made friends—*he just looks like a Pete.*

He does. Something about the eyes, she thinks,
maybe the tongue. Maybe the way he takes it
whole, the mouse, the memory of the other
mice, the sense that there may be something
else out there—another self, another story—
but it's gone before anyone can tell it. This

is the magic of Pete. He makes the world
then swallows it.

SUPERMASSIVE

I stood at the sink and became a few minutes older.

Alive before that moment, alive through the dishes,
then I just kept on with it, left the wet sponge weeping

soap into the drain. I sent Emma a message
with a picture of my face smushed up,

ate grapes and thought about the three possible fates
of the universe: expand forever, expand forever

but slowly, or expand until collapse. All of that
sounded alright. Anyway, what could I do about it?

In close-ups, I think the sun's surface looks like
a Flamin' Hot Cheeto. Lately I feel only hungry,

and fine, and light-years away from myself.

PUT THAT ALL DOWN NOW. BACK AWAY.

Forgive.

Forgive the days their relentless arrival. Accept
their storms as your prophets,

their waters' soft violence.
Forgive the water. Forgive

the clouds their roaming forms.
In another version, oblivion

came for you—more than a passing
notion. Forgive her.

You, you can learn to move on.
See—overhead, the migration:

sandhill cranes spiraling up, up—
harsh, rolling gargle of calls,

crowns the color of rusted blood,
and knife-sharp whitish wings, glinting.

Forgive them. They waste you.

CHAMBERS

Arizona

Everything here is borrowed.

On the other side   of the wall, another
set of walls holding
(their) breath, (no) bodies.

The bed, the beige, the hooks
that held a picture, now missing.

On the other side   of the state line:
Gallup   (which sounds like speed)

still in the swirling sickness.

In the morning, I'll return
my key, leave
                    this room
this place   the next
the next,

pass the highway crosses: Kimberly, Timothy

blank   blank   blank.

Think about the other side,
the missing   (pictures, names)

Everything I thought was mine
is borrowed:
                    breath, body

the rented rooms behind my breastbone—

four chambers, the blood
I left in the sheets.

LIGHTNING SUSPECTED IN DEATHS OF HORSES

I want to take you to the black-mud spring pasture
where six horses fell and did not get back up.
I don't know if they were dark or dappled—
I wasn't there. I read it in a newspaper in Vermont,
sitting at the counter of a diner that no longer
exists. *Lightning Suspected in Deaths of Horses*—
small article in a bottom corner, not much
more information than that. It struck me—
I'm not trying to be funny—I carried
that headline around until it became a slogan,
although I'm not sure what I'd been sold.
Maybe this: the sky opens, you kneel
and beg its mercy, and it doesn't make
one lick of difference. Or maybe, light appears
and your life is transformed. Finally getting
exactly what you asked for all along:
a shift in luck, sudden brilliance, your body
lit, electric, your own enough to let it go.

II.

THE HAWK

A dying man flew west to visit his daughter. They drove
out of town together, then drove back. The daughter
wrote things in a notebook, the man adjusted his seat.
He had trouble getting comfortable, since the cancer
lived in his leg's marrow. They passed a rock face where
someone had graffitied, *SOME PEOPLE CARE TOO MUCH,*
beneath which someone else had added, *It's called love.*
The daughter wrote this down in her notebook. The man
side-eyed the driver of a passing truck, lifted
two fingers in greeting. He said, "Sometimes
when I'm traveling, I get a feeling like I could be home,
and that guy in his truck would still be right there.
I'd be all the way in Cape Cod, and this guy
would be driving his Ford past Drummond, Montana,
either way." She crossed out a word and looked at her father.
"Like, it doesn't matter whether you're here or not?"
The father nodded. He seemed pleased, almost happy.
She felt, for a moment, like she knew him.
"He'd be in his truck, that hawk over there
would fly over that mountain, and I'd be
in Buzzard's Bay, where it'd be raining, or something."
The daughter looked to the sky for his hawk.
It circled and circled, massive wings never flapping.
It was not a hawk, she realized, but a vulture.
It dipped behind the tree line to make good
of some nameless death, and they drove on.

CASSIOPEIA

Meanwhile, a stranger's grandma spoons cold
butterscotch pudding to her lips beside your own grandma.

They prefer custard but won't complain to the nurses.
Revolutions happen elsewhere. The once beloved's face

becomes unfamiliar, the moustache greasier, and it is the least
you could have hoped for, but it doesn't satisfy.

Your brother is doing well because you have adjusted
your definition of "well." He wakes sober in a house

of sober men. They eat dry toast, and he drives to the tiny
Cape Cod airport to wave his arms around and drag

cigarettes, the weight of himself, and duffel bags
filled with souvenir driftwood and bathing suits

along the tarmac all day. The Vineyard people offer
pinched smiles to his dropped *R's* and the desire to feel

another, very particular way plays beneath each
moment like Muzak. He resists. How noble,

to resist. How unlike the gods. Meanwhile, the mortals
are fasting. Your sister listens to the same screech

on repeat and walks along the White River, seeing

only the stones beneath the low, clear water, surprised

by its sting when she kneels and leans to press
her face against their shine. She has not cut her thighs

in weeks. And you go on not calling your brother
or grandmother, crying each time you fold clothes.

Elsewhere, sickness spreading is one way bodies
communicate. Your mother sends a card

with some money in it, says her husband is dying
so slowly he seems fine. You make the same corn salad

for a different set of dinner guests, put on *Nebraska*
one more time. Meanwhile, the constellations. Cassiopeia

hanging upside down from her throne and you on Earth
just gawking, wondering what kind of person you are,

and if you'd be the one to open up your arms
when she's no longer able to hold on.

TIME SURE FLIES WHEN YOU'RE NOT LIVING UP TO YOUR POTENTIAL

So, everything failed. The jabbed-iron trees flamed out
in spectacular failure along the ragged range. Forecast
failed. The pollster that glistered turned huckster. And
the memory of that ex who called you *petit bouchon*
failed to reassure that you once loved wreckful and reckless
and in a foreign tongue. All around you now, Florida fails pinkly
and by voracious flora. The lizard who burned or drowned
hottubbing in your hot coffee failed perfectly, curled into
an eternal question mark, little fingers clenched, dukes up.
If death is the body's failure, it is also its final *fuck you*.
Which has to count for something. Which has to be a win.

"YOU'RE IN FOR A NICE SURPRISE"

In another version, the restaurant doesn't
shut down. Jeff gets new teeth, and Kristina
replaces the money before she gets caught.
Mo quits dealing and Katie ditches Jesus.
Hillary is at peace with her body and doesn't
chew ice chips for warmth. Nicole
isn't fired for informing customers
they're being racist, and the woman who dines
daily on early-bird eggs does not die of MS.
Someone other than my mother orders
the green stuff, so we don't have to trudge
bundled into the back freezer to powerscoop
pistachio until our arms go numb. Nobody
calls the dishwasher "dumb." I don't pick up
smoking so I can sit five minutes alone
on a milk crate, betting which pigeon
gets the fat half of the fry. The day I drive
to a cryptic all-staff meeting, someone gives
the hitchhiker I pass on 140 a ride,
and when I arrive, there's no crane taking
down the sign. The meeting is not to tell us
we're over, but rather, we're all getting raises,
and they want us all to test some new flavors!
And when the hitchhiker comes to the carry-out
window, I don't watch him count quarters
for a cone just to tell him we're closed
forever. I just give it to him. I already
know what he wants, and he's happy.

STRANGER DANGER

Mist makes the trees look grim. Unfamiliar. I still
haven't called my mother. *Are you abducted?*
she writes. *Or kidnapped?* I watch children
climb the hill home, content in their solitude.
Not fearful. *Is there a difference?* I write back.
Also: hello. I'm alive. When I was a child
and unable to sleep, she would read me *The Dangers
of Strangers*, pigtailed girl on the cover, red
ribboned, paused at the knob behind which lurks
the shadowy figure of a man. Inside, strangers
with candy and vans, lost puppies. She had me
recite our address and spell my last name
until my lids grew heavy. Outside lurked
coyotes, mostly, my older brother sneaking
cigarettes behind the garage, young mouth set
tight in a bleak line, squinting towards the ancient
bodies of the trees, the little creek that never rose
except to flood. He was a child, then. As much
as he ever was—maybe thirteen. He crept
wounded through the wet woods, caught bugs.
He feared nothing except being unloved. *And,*
he says now, *vans. All vans. Tinted windows.*
I tell him *No kidding*, say, *now add to that most men.*
We are grown, but we're still her children,
and I believe now it wasn't dying we dreaded
but being drawn away from her, the woman
who had known too many monsters to believe
in safety, who told us their shapes as if knowing

could protect us. As if anything could protect us
but her. *Kidnapped,* she writes, *is usually
for ransom. I would stand a chance of getting
you back.* Outside, the trees loom gray
over a girl stepping from the drawn mouth
of a school van, unscathed, beribboned, bone-
brittle branches swept down as if to hug or clutch.
Abducted, she writes, *no chance—*

GREETINGS: EARTHLINGS, GRETCHEN

We know the difference between contact
and attack, between the way one touches
a hot ladle's handle and the way one handles
a harp. Resound, bewail: the copper hair
of the neighbor who always said *Greetings*
in greeting, her name was Gretchen, every
atom in her seemed alien, vibed green.
She wrote my mother letters—*I worry*
and *Watch your man*. But she was friendly.
She tried to make contact. Cucumbers
from her garden, still prickly, we bristled
at her kindness, trained not to trust
such *truthers*, we mocked her: *Greetings,*
greetings Earthlings, may I use your weeder?
But the truth is, the truth was something
we couldn't handle, hands over our eyes
but peeping through the middle. Then
one day she was gone, sick-bright grass
where her garden had been. Our family
remained as we were but strange: strangers.

WHEN I WAS AN ALCHEMIST I DISCOVERED NOTHING

The world outside is dead and dark November—

the month of my earthly arrival. The Saxons

called it *Blotmonad*—blood month, a time for sacrifice.

Inside, I cover eggplant in wet, red sauce. Nightshade

on nightshade, the spices on my fingertips a fine

powdered gold. What gods remain have quit

taking bribes. I cut my thumb paring carrots

and call it blessing, *blessure*. Knowledge

is a tree, yes, but merely. Twigs stabbing up

to bleed the sky. I don't believe in dividing

the planet by four. I believe in salting eggplant

slices. In leeching bruised, bitter water

from their flesh. Who will I thank for this?

I am alone in the kitchen, sharpening a knife.

IGUANA IGUANA

Key West

Things crawl over me here, no-see-ums and biting
ants. They make me feel hospitable, like at last
I am a good host. *Stop itching*, I tell myself,
we have guests. What is a guest if not something
that takes a little bit of your life? In the cemetery
where I practice pedaling, sailing circles around
the dead, iguanas sun bake and scurry the white
slabs, the green length of them defiant drapery
in death's pale parlor. I'm told they're invasive—
even their taxonomy, *iguana iguana,* it's too much,
too many iguanas, the William Carlos Williams
of reptiles, or the man my mother loved after
my father, Jim James, who chugged caffeine-free
Diet Pepsi and made his pecs dance, recited
the three words of Italian he learned from Sylvester
Stallone (*Ti amo* and *andiamo).* He once argued
with me over my stubborn belief that ten thousand
was the same thing as one million. I was never good
with numbers. He was never good with kids.
He built things and made my mother laugh. Maybe
too much. Maybe for the wrong reasons. During cold
snaps, the iguanas freeze and fall like stoned fruit
from the trees, wake only once their core
has warmed. I won't be here to see it—it's the off-
season now, August, everything dank and hot-
-blooded, which is what I think my mother
liked about Jim: something raw about him,

the pink scars where his own mother's
boyfriend stubbed out cigarettes on his arms
or how he called *Here kitty kitty* nightly
into the dark after the cat ran away.
She was a stray to begin with—we lured her
into our lives with milk, named her Fitty Fat
the Kitty Kat, let her eat and fuck and kill
as much as she wanted, litters of kittens
and kibble and dead birds piling up.
What else is there to say but everything
we've said before, over and again? *Iguana iguana.*
Italian Stallion. Here, kitty kitty. Andiamo,
Jim James. What is a child if not something
that takes a little bit of your life? He wasn't
a bad man. He made my mother laugh.

GOAT THINGS

When Trish calls and reminds me that someone

who gives freely and happily is called *generous,*

I think of the man on the mountain who watches

and walks with the panting band of dusty goats.

His name is Sam. The goats have names like Joy

and Compassion. Intuition. One walks over here

and chews a bit of sagebrush. One stares at me

with horizontal pupils—useful for head-hung,

hunted creatures. I'm not sure what joy is

to a goat. Seeing everything? The good, tough

sage leaves. I remember, then, a boy I knew

whose family goat boxed the breath from his body

with a quick kick to the chest. Not compassionate.

Not *not* compassionate. Goats do goat things,

whatever those are. What are we good for?

I mean, to each other. Why do we do that?

GAZE

And the hillside branded with cattle, each dark

crown bowed to the grass, dutiful and unaware

of duty. Just one of the herd with his head up,

a calf looking in my direction, across the pasture,

across the road, standing by my car, recently oiled,

recently wrecked. Not long for this world. And he

is not looking at me, nor beyond me, just looking.

And I remember being younger, talking to a friend

at a loud and expensive bar in Boston about the mind's

bright machine and our species' good fortune.

She sucked wing sauce off her thumb and said, *Yes,*

but cows don't kill themselves. Maybe she wasn't

my friend. Or she was disturbed by my desire to know

her, my eyes' constant feeding. Maybe the last time

we saw one another I saw nothing but the angus-black

rope of her long hair, which I pulled taut and toward me.

TWISTER

I always want to start with, *it wasn't*—it wasn't
this, but *this*. It wasn't like *that*. The girl,
not the gown. The gall, not the girl.
It wasn't so bad. It wasn't like *that*. The past,
not the moment. The tongue, not the twister.
The orange, not the pith, the oblivion,
not the forgotten thing. It was green,
but not like tarnished copper. It was green,
like light underwater. Like water with light
going through it: green, like the algae, not
the water, like the thing between her teeth,
not the back tooth in need of a root canal.
How do I show you? No, not you—*you*?
The web, not the spider, the twister, not her
farmhouse dinner. Green light, green sky.
The acid, not the rain. The moon, not
the lunatic river. I wasn't like that. I'm not
what you're thinking. Green light, baby.
Not me, not the gone thing, glinting.

NOT THE FLY BUT THE AMBER

I like to sit and watch things rot. Twin
sunflowers in an empty bourbon bottle,

fuzzy mold turtlenecking their stems.
I am muscle and husk, the wrong
way to talk to your mother. Sugar
is a falseness. Lollipops and hard candies

are all called suckers for a reason. A tidal
wave of molasses once crashed over Boston.

Twelve dead. Now, people play bocce
where others were crystalized like ancient

bloodsuckers stuck in resin. A gesture
from my sweetheart, the flowers, too,

look embalmed. Their lion heads forever
downcast as if Pompeiied in a hangdog

moment. I hold the bottle to the honeyed
light just so, swirl the dry dead inside.

They say decay smells sickly sweet.
I don't want to be a sucker, throat

clogged tight with syrup. I want to be
the glut and glug of a slow flood, a body

unrolled and blooming, the scent
of burnt sugar still haunting the streets.

KNOWING

I watched the fog pool in. From where I stood
on the path I could see a dog, a lab mix, rush
to his person on the field below. At my feet
on the path stood my own dog, merengue-white,
and all around us the fog, smoke-white and curling
up like a French inhale, then sinking like the end
of something, a day or a drowning, peaceful,
unasked-for but not unwanted. It moved toward us
without motive or hurry. It covered the world.
The person, the dog, the field, the dog, the person,
the path, the lodge poles, thin and high like
a querulous voice, thin and high like my younger
self, blowing smoke rings—I never learned
to French inhale—that undid themselves in the gray
air above my bed then sank, dissolved. In the years
since then, I have become someone else.
I have never left that room. I have slipped
unnoticed into the woods, have been surrounded.
And in the years since then I have known weather,
have stepped from an open door into the thick
and settled vapor, have driven through ghosts
of it on dark mountain roads. But today I thought,
Isn't it something—to see for once what was coming
until it overcame me, until I was overcome.

CRYSTAL BALL

I don't see myself

in the smoked quartz orb

of the moon.

I see myself in the daytime

winter sky. Gray

blank. I see myself

in the hawk's eyes:

another dashing

creature.

Today is taking walk-ins—

tonight, not so much.

There you are, I say

to the world

of things

that haven't happened

yet. Knowing

the future

is easy.

We don't exist

there. I think that

about covers it.

A PILGRIM IS A FOREIGNER

As for encounters with the divine, I have not thought
of counting seagulls nor the night I tripped mushrooms
and forgave my father, but rather of a plain quivering rabbit
who once appeared before me as a bell clanged midnight.
I have watched the hail make chaos of the maple leaves
and remembered that ruin means there is something enough
to destroy. I have thought to doom a nest-flung baby cowbird
by offering the respite of my self-scented palm. There
beneath that tree, outside a bar, the woman who tsk-tsked
my open hand away had bulging eyes, dead with drink. Later on,
a man preached against agnosticism's passivity. He believed
only in the mind's fallibility. Poor logician—
I have a weakness for these types. He drank my whiskey
hot. He left me feeling cold. He confessed a desire to be famous
for making film. I wanted to say, *You cannot make something*
if you believe in nothing, though I had built so many
shrines on doubt. But later, stroking the dark
birthmark on his hip, I thought of brood parasites,
the watchful stealth of mother cowbirds, who hide their eggs
in strangers' nests so they can leave to follow cattle
for their flies. There are untold unseens in which
not to believe. All his wished-for witnesses,
their upturned, screen-lit eyes.

ALL MY EXES LIVE IN THIS POEM

We ditched you once for a big burrito. Then again

for smoked meat and AC. Skipped a date to sip

fishbowls at the mermaid bar, didn't call back

for weeks. Compared your ass to the Rolling

Stones, you're welcome, tried to use it to balance

a glass. Cut our foot on the broken window, bled

into the thread count while you pretended to sleep.

We catalogued each thing you said that you hated:

messy-faced kids and white chocolate, or hearing

our beefy hearts beat. Against our better judgment,

we wrote letters from cold countries: *Dear you, Still*

alive? How's your mother? Still strange? And you?

Still strange? Received word on our thirty-first:

thirty-one cards that all said *Fuck your birth.*

If we failed to fight to keep you, it was because

you were already lost. A sea-like silence alive

at the center of you. It is you and it is more

brutal than you. Killer, it swallowed us all.

WHITEOUT

Like something true, the snow came

and obliterated the world. What I thought

was the world—the pines, the sky,

my wooden walls, the roads that take me

away from myself, the walls, the pines,

farther from and towards the apparent

horizon, invisible now for the snow

falling white from a white expanse.

Once, I wrote my name there, deep

in its body. This is how it found me.

Knew what to call me. It called me.

Calls. I stand under it and let it wipe me

clean from this world. What I thought

was the world were objects in a landscape

slowly painted over until only the painter—

eyes closed, brush thick with the deed—

knew they were there. Are they there?

I stand outside and let it remember me

until nothing, no one else does.

OBLIVION

Maybe sleeping with the river stone smooth

between your breasts was not the best idea.

You believed it held the water's power,

its rush and glacial cold, and you longed

for this. Or maybe you just liked its weight,

like the warm hand of a witch pressing you

asleep. Instead you got the river's fury,

feeling acutely the absence of that precise

stone. This, too, will erode you at the pace

of centuries. Eventually you will become

the smallest pebble, soft to the touch,

smelling of moss. One day, a young man

with smooth hands and a cloudy eye will near

your river's edge. He will find you.

Pluck you. He will plop you into his mouth

and swallow you, because this, poor dreamer

is the world. Nobody escapes.

WE NEVER LIVED IN FLORIDA

We never saw the gators long, as that endless year,

longing to snap us down the middle like a Kit Kat.

Never saw them soaking up the hurricane on the side

of 441, the prairie glutted. Suspicion and doubt never

gutted us like the trout Brett never caught off the coast

of Cedar Key. Nobody said it looked like he was having

a religious experience, deep-fried and shirtless, head

turned to the unforgiving sun, up to his waders in warm

Gulf. There was no religion there. No billboards

for the unborn next to billboards for the "barely legal."

No cartoon seal cub holding a fetus saying, *Save*

the baby humans. We never needed saving, because

that Cassadaga psychic never saw our auras bruised

and bottle-black, never said we'd jump ship within

the year. We didn't. We've been here all along, watching

barges move lethargic down the Ohio River—murky

snake that separates us from Kentucky, birthplace

of our foremothers, who never warned us about

the heat down south or the way the earth sometimes

opens its mouth and swallows folks in that sinking

swamp, which could never—*never*—suck us down.

MARRIAGE

Years now, you have lived
beside the mountain.

Have watched the clouds'
shadows move across

the sage-scrubbed mountain,
and it is like watching

from the sea floor
whales moving

beneath boats.
Breath-holding beings

bending light.
Years now, you have lived

in a cottage cozied up
to the mountain. Years now,

you have known
fuck all

about the mountain.
You know you love

the fog-bearded mountain.
You don't know

exactly what
that means.

CAVEAT

It is not enough to love yourself. It is not enough

to make your throat a slide for warm broth, nor

to have heated stones piled on your back. It is not enough

to be yourself. So be it. Not enough. There are no

good places to live and no good ways to die.

About the too-much-sweet and foggy blossom of the drug

your first love loved best, he said, *Never enough*

and slipped into nothing, the cat licking his slack

face until morning. To say you loved him once,

why bother? He loved you back, but not enough.

It is not enough to love others. To cry at the shape of them

and imagine their insides. They don't like imagining you

imagining their insides. (The gut flora, the mean

little stones amassing malice in the kidneys.) Don't do it.

There isn't enough spit in circulation to shine up

what's tarnished in you, and what's tarnished

isn't tarnished enough. Stop trying. Lay into the world

like it's good enough. It'll have to be. Maybe it is.

III.

THOSE LONG ABSENT ARE COMING BACK TO YOU

You are older now than the one who plunged

into the gorge after three straight weeks

of rain, or the girl dumped there six years before—

the one who'd taught you

they were called *toggle clasps*, her body

unbuttoned to the neck. You've outlived

your first drug dealer and his exotic fish, steady

pulse of aquarium light haloing

the exit wound. They have become unspeakable

names. And you have become

yourself—walking up and down the bridge

in winter empty-handed, no gloves.

So conscious of the river below, swollen with ice,

so cold and definite. And you know

beneath the slabs the stones

are still green and brown, still blue

like eyes frozen open, but you

don't see them. You don't even look.

WE WERE YOUNGER THEN

as we always were, acutely unaware of it.
We were not at home in ourselves. We slept
in the park after missing the ferry. What did we care for?
Whom? Not the suspiciously sober English guy
who took us home when we were too drunk
to stand and had fallen asleep in the closet
on top of the coats. Not the coats—we
were always cold, though we swore we crackled,
swore we burned. Not the pills all our friends
were stitched to back then—some for pain,
some just killers. Every year, the younger self
dissolves like Alka-Seltzer in today's waters,
where we emerge, fizzy-headed, a little more
settled, our hearts less burned, our debts
unpayable. What do those dead regret?
They still call us from the coat closet,
from the park bench and the empty ferry:
get up, get up, get up.

MINTHE

Mint went straight to our heads those days,
surged our veins' green sutures like a drug.

Corn mint. Apple mint.

Miscarried after the derby that year. Your louse
of a love deep in the corn mash, crying.

You did not cry (for)
Kentucky mint. Julep mint.

Mating season coincided with the garden plot's
comeuppance. We panicked our lips red, chewed Orbit.

Spearmint. Peppermint.

You named the baby Miranda and hoped
her silence meant apotheosis,

like that river nymph the dead's queen saved
from loving Hades. She turned her into mint.

We drank less after that. Scotch mint
in our scotchless sodas.

Men drove by like they always did.
The louse was gone.

We planted gravel.
Smoked menthols.

Mostly our lives were glorious.

I DON'T KNOW WHAT PEOPLE SHOULD DO

I'm sitting in the backyard: fire pit, night's thinnest hours.
Next door, a baby crying. The sound
so alien to my life I mistake it for a tomcat—
hot need beneath the neighbors' rusted out-trampolines, feral
pleading. Assumptions
about what we couldn't possibly understand
are cobbled together from what little we do.
Like last week, when I saw an elderly couple holding hands
and believed they were having an affair.
I've been told that love doesn't always start in darkness,
but I can't tell you for certain. A man's voice booms
from inside the neighbors' house FUCK *OFF*
and the baby stops for a minute,
then starts again.
Not the brightest beginning to a life,
but there it is. Elsewhere in the valley:
dream of the old couple stretching feline across her bed,
a gold bracelet skimming
talc-powdered skin he tried not to love, threatening
to slip off her wrist.
They are satisfied. Humming
and irreparable. Standing at the edge
of their lives, astonished
at how much they have carried. The weight
of knowing and missing whoever they were,
already losing whoever they are.
Not to mention the others. Not to mention
the illicit agony of watching
a fire pit empty its smoke up into the sky
like a middle finger
to the still-burning stars. Or gold falling
softly to the floor.

CEDAR KEY

Bayside, two women sit in the sand. They click
pictures of one another, of the sea just beyond.
All three bodies reflect the light. Brine-shimmer,

skin-shimmer, shrine of something inside. One
rests her head on the other's warmed shoulder,
then lies down. The other hands her a T-shirt

to cover her eyes. Nearby docks bear signs
advising fishermen to do just this to the unlucky
pelicans caught by their lures, to soothe with

not seeing, with soft cloth over the eyes. The two
women are already serene, savoring the sights,
the not-seeing, the closeness of the other. This is

love, or friendship, which is also love. Meanwhile,
the sand gives over to form and remains, somehow,
itself. I want to be shaped and unshaped like that. But also

to stay firm like the oyster shells I pull from the surf—
some fused together, ridged blue as if veined, fixed
forever to the first hard surface they touch. I want

a form that is a home I can leave and return to. I want
to use my cells to build a fortress, then tear the fortress
down. If I pledge allegiance to my body, I will never be

homesick, though I may always be at war. You can't cut free
a pelican until you remove the hook that took her in—
What brought me here? By what lure? When the women

loosen themselves from the shore, they are different.
They don't know it. They shake out their blankets, scatter
former castles. When they leave I am different.

They don't know me. Their voices rise and fall
like water, like the cool tongue of the world lapping
senseless her own great, unsolvable wound.

BETTER HOMES AND GARDENS

Whiteflies in the tomato plant, yawning gauze

of spider mite web in the mint. Thumb-sized

roach over the doorway like a talisman. Smashed

it—bad luck? Can't unclog the bathtub. Tried

Coca-Cola, hot vinegar, snakes. Now everything

hissing. Now pissing rain all through the night.

Dirt smell, warm and wet. Swamp mist. Palmetto

sounds like an old-timey cocktail. Toss it back.

Pretend the earth is yours, like you bought it

outright, no layaway, no loans. Like it isn't just

waiting to open, reclaim you. Like it doesn't

know already exactly when and how it will.

RICOCHET

Where one should hear the echo of a duck's call
there is only glazed stillness, the word *lake* so close
to *lacquer lack*. Stood at the scum-rimmed edge,
I said *nothing*, a friend said *listen*, but I only heard
a recollection: elsewhere, ice cube cracking in glass
and the reddest juice poured high, blooming in vodka.
Thinking of all the great plunges. Of old men in frozen
oceans, necklines, Icarus. Descent, like mallard call,
given to narrowing. How desperate we are for what
recedes. That friend on the lake shore, how she used
her hands to mimic the waterfowl and how they lifted
quickly from the surface, alarmed by the false reflection.
Then the plaid blur of her, taking off. When this
comes back to me, something darkens as she calls
to them—shadows of speechless creatures
somehow alighting on her face.

MICHELLE PFEIFFER IS MAKING SOMETHING OF A COMEBACK

at least on the radio, but I just keep
listening to *Tusk*. Receive it
like a reaping. Heart-hooked,
sickled by brass. Elsewhere,
the grass grows tall
and gets cut. Grows tall and gets
cut. Nobody
thinks about it. The earth's slow
metronome of days
beating on. Tusk. Tusk.
Tusk. Michelle Pfeiffer says,
Love humiliates you.
Hatred cradles you,
and I have been humiliated
by love, but hatred does not
cradle me, unless
you count America,
in whose hate-filled heartland
I am held, waiting
for something like a comeback
or at least to sign a new lease.
I eat too-sour berries
and wince with pleasure, walk
the country road and racket
my fingers along the corn stalks
like a prisoner rattles a cup
along the bars of her cell
or a baby rattles a toy
along the bars of her crib.
Stevie sings,
But when you build your house,

then call me home.
So I Godzilla deeper
into the great, gold-green height,
and I name this stampede *harvest*
and I name this ruin *house*
and I stand inside my doorframe, calling.

ALTER EGOS TALK BACK

Oh, her. We know about that one, all right.
Skulking through her "real life" like a thief.

She has taken everything from us. Every
almost existence, each one as real as hers.

But we go on in our elsewhere. We tend
the garden she dug then ditched

in Missoula. We feed the Boston fern
she forgot in the Cincinnati garage.

It's alive. It's thriving. It's amazing
what you can do with a little light

and attention—who knew.
(We did. She did too.)

We go back to the gallery in Gainesville
with the winged girl from Bumble,

and we don't feel any smarter,
and we don't cause any trouble.

We remain unsure of what to say
            about art   or the living

so we walk around, nodding, going *cool
that's so cool,*   and it's enough.

We try. We stave off the blankness
beckoning, keep the faith. We do

what she didn't, what she couldn't:
we stay.

THE WILDING

The town was covered in houses like a body of scaling bandages,
gluey and obscene.

We set ours on a hill.

Spread the beds with chenille, avoided the rustling
of neighbors. We painted our eyelashes
shut. Still,

the townspeople wagged their tongues, steepling
them towards that apron of blue light,
not heaven,

an abattoir of unanswerables:

I don't believe we've met.

And we buttered ourselves against each other, the "good fat,"
the bad apples, we sliced into them,

rife with worms, we didn't care,
we grew guttural

and older. We escaped cultivation. We flannelled
our necks, necked, let our hair grow

wilding, spotted ourselves
in ourselves less and less frequently.

Some days we stepped from the ether of each other into the skinned mink of others, their boudoirs lamp-lit and gauzy with moving shadow.

We loved them, somehow. We returned to each other new.

PRESENT CONDITIONAL

If, in the wet, dead grass,
newly exposed,

      there are small, brown pellets,
a deer once stood in that spot.

And if a deer once stood in that spot,
I know there are reasons to stand

      (in the once-garden, overgrown
      with relics)

and that others have known this too.

If something is broken
within me, it is not

the most vital part.

There are keys in my pocket.

Somewhere else,
an opening.

TURNING

So you return to the Rattlesnake in the rattling

old Ford, hit twice this summer and stinking

of sour milk. The pines and larches pierce

you to needles, their spines black and limbs

spidering yellow, ballooning green & thick

over the hills. It is a fine day. You feel fine

& fine spreads its gauze over the valley's

deep gouge, seals it off. You can breathe

in the trembling stand,

                can tongue fresh copper

from the rip in your knee. Quake. For you will

be older soon. & you know

                you are already. & the little

coins of aspen leaf are still half living,

& the dead half flicks its gold on & off

              like ghosts at the switch,

the windows of your life lit long enough

for you to see them as they close.

ACKNOWLEDGMENTS

Grateful acknowledgment to the editors of the following journals in which versions of these poems first appeared, sometimes under different titles:

"Passage" first appeared in *Crazyhorse*, and was reprinted on *Verse Daily*

"Window" and "Spring-loaded" first appeared in *Tinderbox Poetry Journal*

"For My Twenty-Year-Old Sister on my Thirtieth Birthday" first appeared in *Washington Square Review*

"Crosscut," "Minthe," and "Goat Things," first appeared in *The Pinch*

"One Way" and "Gaze" first appeared in *Willow Springs*

"The Funny Part" first appeared in in *Fugue*

"Supermassive" first appeared in *Denver Quarterly*

"Lightning Suspected in Deaths of Horses" and "Time Sure Flies When You're Not Living Up to Your Potential" first appeared in *Four Way Review*

"Cassiopeia" first appeared in *New England Review*

"The Hawk" first appeared in *Cimarron Review*

"Not the Fly but the Amber" and "All My Exes Live in This Poem" first appeared in *Passages North*

"Iguana Iguana" first appeared in *Raleigh Review*, where it was awarded the 2019 Laux/Millar Prize

"A Pilgrim Is a Foreigner" first appeared in *Salt Hill*

"I Don't Know What People Should Do" first appeared in *The Louisville Review*, where it was awarded the 2016 Louisville Literary Arts Writer's Block Prize for Poetry

"Marriage" first appeared in *Western Humanities Review*

"Caveat" first appeared in *The Journal*

"Those Long Absent Are Coming Back to You" first appeared in *The Portland Review*

"Cedar Key" first appeared in *Pleiades*

"Better Homes and Gardens" first appeared in *Hot Metal Bridge*

"Ricochet" first appeared in *Salamander*

"Michelle Pfeiffer Is Making Something of a Comeback" first appeared in *Third Coast*

"The Wilding" first appeared in *Ghost Town*

"Turning" first appeared in *Blue Earth Review*

Thank you to Sebastián Páramo for finding the heart of this book and shepherding it into the world, for your keen insights and thoughtful feedback, and for your faith and enthusiasm. Thank you to Will Evans and the Deep Vellum staff for all the work you do to build a home for so many books. Thank you, Zoe Norvell, for taking a very chaotic Pinterest board and translating it into the perfect, scaly cover.

Thank you to my poetry teachers: Sherwin Bitsui, Gabriel Fried, David Huddle, Joanna Klink, Prageeta Sharma, and Karen Volkman. There is no unit by which to measure how much your minds, time, and care have meant to me. You have given me an invaluable gift. Thank you.

Thank you to the following institutions, which have supported my writing: The University of Vermont, the University of Montana, the University of Missouri, the Vermont Studio Center, The Studios of Key West, and Idyllwild Arts Academy. Thank you in particular to Kim Henderson, tireless department maestro and superb teaching artist, as well as the preternaturally talented creative writers at Idyllwild Arts Academy—many happy saxophones for you. Birchard forever!

Thank you to my students, past and present, who have taught me so much about writing, reading, and staying curious about the world. Working with you has been the privilege of my life.

Thank you to the poets Mackenzie Cole, Allison Linville, Rachel Mindell, Alicia Mountain, and Phil Schaefer for poemathons, kinship, friendship, spirit, and heart. And poems. Thank you to Shea Boresi, Chelsea Fabian, Paul Lee, and Cheryl Weatherby for your thoughtful feedback on this manuscript's most recent poems.

Thank you, Alicia Mountain and Emma Quaytman, for the smushed faces and fierce friendship that have sustained me and thus my writing. Thank you, Tricia T. Santoro, for being my first literary collaborator and for decades of laughs and weirdness. Thank you to Allison Stevens for your endless generosity, support, and good dog pictures.

Thank you, Matt Aizenstadt, Robert Downey, Ryan Headley, Johanna Hiller, Marissa Lee, Suzanne Lunden, Christa Pagliei, Anthony Parshall, Mike Wheeler, Ryan Winnick, and the rest of BPS for accepting me into the fold of our first writing community—and for all the wine. Let's take that train someday.

I have had the good fortune of growing up with families that value art, humor, and stories. To my mother, Judy Capra-Petercuskie, thank you for your unwavering love and support, for always reading, for not getting too weirded out by the poems, and for all the trips to the library and the bookstore. You made me a reader, and thus a writer. Thank you to my stepfather, John, for your support of this admittedly puzzling pursuit. Thank you to my brother Curtis for your generous spirit and madcap humor. Thank you to my nephew Clayton for brightening the world with your presence. Thank you to my father, Marc Thomas, for passing on to me your love of narrative and for tuning my ear to music. I gave up on playing, but I hear it in language. Thank you to my stepmother, Lisa, for modeling lifelong creative engagement. Thank you to my sister Madison "Madge" Ruth, for the good car ideas, kinship, and laughter. Thank you to my sister Rileigh for inspiring me with your kindness and strength of spirit, and to my brother Jake for lols and snackspiration. Thank you to my aunties Cindy and Nancy for your love and support.

Thank you to Billy Bones Wallace for reading every draft, tirelessly rooting for me, and for keeping me supplied with snacks—and love, which is also snacks. Thank you for the fun, creativity, and warmth of our life together. Thank you to Bear and Frankie for the snugs, fun, and pure, uncomplicated, unconditional love.

Thank you to all the poets who came before me, to all the poets who are writing now, and to all the poets who aren't here yet. Thank you for your poems, and for sharing with me the weight, wonder, strangeness, and high-wire thrill of this art.

And thank you, reader. What is any of this without you? I can't believe these poems have made it into your hands. They're yours now—with love.

CAYLIN CAPRA-THOMAS'S other works include the chapbooks *Inside My Electric City* (YesYes Books) and *The Marilyn Letters* (dancing girl press). Her poems have appeared in journals including *New England Review, Pleiades, Copper Nickel, 32 Poems, Hayden's Ferry Review,* and many others. The 2018-2020 poet-in-residence at Idyllwild Arts Academy, she now lives in Columbia, Missouri, where she is a PhD student in English and creative writing.

Thank you all
for your support.
We do this for you,
and could not do
it without you.

DEEP
VELLUM

PARTNERS

ALLRED
CAPITAL MANAGEMENT
of
RAYMOND JAMES®

ADDITIONAL DONORS, CONT'D

Mark Haber

Mary Cline

Maynard Thomson

Michael Reklis

Mike Soto

Mokhtar Ramadan

Nikki & Dennis Gibson

Patrick Kukucka

Patrick Kutcher

Rev. Elizabeth & Neil Moseley

Richard Meyer

Scott & Katy Nimmons

Sherry Perry

Sydneyann Binion

Stephen Harding

Stephen Williamson

Susan Carp

Susan Ernst

Theater Jones

Tim Perttula

Tony Thomson

SUBSCRIBERS

Margaret Terwey

Ben Fountain

Gina Rios

Elena Rush

Courtney Sheedy

Caroline West

Brian Bell

Charles Dee Mitchell

Cullen Schaar

Harvey Hix

Jeff Lierly

Elizabeth Simpson

Nicole Yurcaba

Jennifer Owen

Melanie Nicholls

Alan Glazer

Michael Doss

Matt Bucher

Katarzyna Bartoszynska

Michael Binkley

Erin Kubatzky

Martin Piñol

Michael Lighty

Joseph Rebella

Jarratt Willis

Heustis Whiteside

Samuel Herrera

Heidi McElrath

Jeffrey Parker

Carolyn Surbaugh

Stephen Fuller

Kari Mah

Matt Ammon

Elif Ağanoğlu

AVAILABLE NOW FROM DEEP VELLUM

SHANE ANDERSON · *After the Oracle* · USA

MICHÈLE AUDIN · *One Hundred Twenty-One Days* · translated by Christiana Hills · FRANCE

BAE SUAH · *Recitation* · translated by Deborah Smith · SOUTH KOREA

MARIO BELLATIN · *Mrs. Murakami's Garden* · translated by Heather Cleary · *Beauty Salon* · translated by David Shook · MEXICO

EDUARDO BERTI · *The Imagined Land* · translated by Charlotte Coombe · ARGENTINA

CARMEN BOULLOSA · *Texas: The Great Theft* · *Before* · *Heavens on Earth* translated by Samantha Schnee · Peter Bush · Shelby Vincent · MEXICO

MAGDA CARNECI · *FEM* · translated by Sean Cotter · ROMANIA

LEILA S. CHUDORI · *Home* · translated by John H. McGlynn · INDONESIA

MATHILDE CLARK · *Lone Star* · translated by Martin Aitken · DENMARK

SARAH CLEAVE, ed. · *Banthology: Stories from Banned Nations* · IRAN, IRAQ, LIBYA, SOMALIA, SUDAN, SYRIA & YEMEN

LOGEN CURE · *Welcome to Midland: Poems* · USA

ANANDA DEVI · *Eve Out of Her Ruins* · translated by Jeffrey Zuckerman · MAURITIUS

PETER DIMOCK · *Daybook from Sheep Meadow* · USA

CLAUDIA ULLOA DONOSO · *Little Bird*, translated by Lily Meyer · PERU/NORWAY

RADNA FABIAS · *Habitus* · translated by David Colmer · CURAÇAO/NETHERLANDS

ROSS FARRAR · *Ross Sings Cheree & the Animated Dark: Poems* · USA

ALISA GANIEVA · *Bride and Groom* · *The Mountain and the Wall* translated by Carol Apollonio · RUSSIA

FERNANDA GARCIA LAU · *Out of the Cage* · translated by Will Vanderhyden · ARGENTINA

ANNE GARRÉTA · *Sphinx* · *Not One Day* · *In/concrete* · translated by Emma Ramadan · FRANCE

JÓN GNARR · *The Indian* · *The Pirate* · *The Outlaw* · translated by Lytton Smith · ICELAND

GOETHE · *The Golden Goblet: Selected Poems* · *Faust, Part One* translated by Zsuzsanna Ozsváth and Frederick Turner · GERMANY

SARA GOUDARZI · *The Almond in the Apricot* · USA

NOEMI JAFFE · *What are the Blind Men Dreaming?* · translated by Julia Sanches & Ellen Elias-Bursac · BRAZIL

CLAUDIA SALAZAR JIMÉNEZ · *Blood of the Dawn* · translated by Elizabeth Bryer · PERU

PERGENTINO JOSÉ · *Red Ants* · MEXICO

TAISIA KITAISKAIA · *The Nightgown & Other Poems* · USA

SONG LIN · *The Gleaner Song: Selected Poems* · translated by Dong Li · CHINA

JUNG YOUNG MOON · *Seven Samurai Swept Away in a River* · *Vaseline Buddha* translated by Yewon Jung · SOUTH KOREA

KIM YIDEUM · *Blood Sisters* · translated by Ji yoon Lee · SOUTH KOREA

JOSEFINE KLOUGART · *Of Darkness* · translated by Martin Aitken · DENMARK

YANICK LAHENS · *Moonbath* · translated by Emily Gogolak · HAITI